# Who Was
# Celia Cruz?

by Pam Pollack and Meg Belviso

illustrated by Jake Murray

Penguin Workshop

Para Roberto Ponce Vargas—PP

For Cara—MB

For Tracy—thank you for using the gift
of your voice to bring some joy to those
around you during difficult times—JM

PENGUIN WORKSHOP
An Imprint of Penguin Random House LLC, New York

If you purchased this book without a cover, you should be aware that this book is stolen
property. It was reported as "unsold and destroyed" to the publisher, and neither the author
nor the publisher has received any payment for this "stripped book."

Penguin supports copyright. Copyright fuels creativity, encourages diverse voices, promotes
free speech, and creates a vibrant culture. Thank you for buying an authorized edition of
this book and for complying with copyright laws by not reproducing, scanning,
or distributing any part of it in any form without permission. You are supporting
writers and allowing Penguin to continue to publish books for every reader.

The publisher does not have any control over and does not assume any responsibility
for author or third-party websites or their content.

Copyright © 2020 by Penguin Random House LLC. All rights reserved.
Published by Penguin Workshop, an imprint of Penguin Random House LLC, New York.
PENGUIN and PENGUIN WORKSHOP are trademarks of Penguin Books Ltd.
WHO HQ & Design is a registered trademark of Penguin Random House LLC.
Printed in the USA.

Visit us online at www.penguinrandomhouse.com.

Library of Congress Control Number: 2019054705

ISBN 9780448488691 (paperback)        10 9 8 7 6 5 4 3
ISBN 9781524792138 (library binding)    10 9 8 7 6 5 4 3 2 1

# Contents

# Who Was Celia Cruz?

One Saturday morning in 1947 in Havana, Cuba, Celia Cruz woke up early. It was an exciting day. Earlier that week, her cousin Serafín had surprised her by signing her up for a singing contest. He thought his cousin was talented enough to win.

The contest was for a radio show called *La hora del té* (say: la OR-a del TAY), which means "teatime." Celia loved listening to the show. Her whole family did. Celia was twenty-two years old and had loved to sing all her life, but she had never appeared onstage or on the radio. She looked out at her family's backyard and all the other houses on her street. Everything was covered in dew. Celia thought it made her neighborhood sparkle like a sequined gown.

She put on a white dress, white tights, and nice white shoes. Her mother combed her dark hair into a bun and fastened it with a beautiful clip. Then Celia and Serafín got on the bus that would take them the twelve blocks to the radio station. In her hands Celia held her claves (say: KLA-vays), wooden sticks that she tapped together to keep the beat while she sang.

When they got to the radio station, there were many other contestants waiting. Most of them were older than Celia. When it was her turn, she sang a song called "Nostalgia," tapping her claves as she sang. Once she started to sing, Celia stopped thinking about the other contestants and the competition. She just enjoyed the song. She was completely surprised when she won first prize.

For first prize, Celia was given a cake from one of the best bakeries in Havana. When she and Serafín got back on the bus, they placed the cake box carefully on their laps so it would not get crushed. Their family was very poor. They had never had a cake in such a fancy box. They couldn't wait to get home to look at it, so they opened the box on the bus.

The cake was covered in white frosting with colorful flowers. It was so delicate, it seemed to be made of lace. Celia and Serafín enjoyed the cake's delicious smell before closing the box again.

When they got home, Celia found her whole family waiting for her on the porch. They cheered when they saw her. She opened the box, and everyone shared the beautiful cake. Celia never forgot how good it tasted.

It wasn't just winning that felt good. Celia had loved singing in the contest. She couldn't wait to do it again. She didn't know that one day she would sing for crowds all over the world.

# CHAPTER 1
## Lullabies and Carnival

Celia Cruz was born in Havana, Cuba, on October 21, 1925. Her full name was Úrsula Hilaria Celia Caridad Cruz Alfonso. Her father was Simón Cruz, and her mother was Catalina Alfonso, but everyone called her Ollita.

# Cuba

The Republic of Cuba is the largest island in the Caribbean. Havana is its capital city. The island sits in the spot where the Caribbean Sea, the Atlantic Ocean, and the Gulf of Mexico meet, south of the US state of Florida.

The original people of Cuba were the Native American Ciboney and Taino. The island was

conquered by the Spanish in the late fifteenth century. It was a Spanish colony until 1898 when it became independent after the Spanish-American War.

Cuba is a country with many kinds of people. They include descendants of the original Taino and Ciboney, white descendants of the Spanish, and descendants of enslaved black people brought there from Africa and other islands in the Caribbean.

The neighborhood she lived in was very poor. Most of the people who lived there, including Celia and her family, were black. They were Afro-Cuban, descended from African people who had been enslaved and brought to Cuba by the Spanish who settled there in the late fifteenth century.

Celia and her family were very close. She was the second oldest of four children. She had an older sister, Dolores, a brother, Bárbaro, and a younger sister, Gladys. One of Celia's aunts, Tía Ana, often treated her like a daughter.

Many people lived in the small house in the Santos Suárez district in Havana. The family included not just Celia, her parents, and her siblings but also her grandmother and many other relatives. Celia's mother often sang while she cooked traditional Cuban dishes like white rice and black beans, papaya and fried ripe plantains, and *ropa vieja* (say: ROPE-a vee-AY-ha), a beef stew whose name means "old clothes."

Everyone had chores to do. As she got older, one of Celia's was to put all the younger children to bed each night. She had to give them their bath and put them to sleep. Once they were tucked in, she always sang them a lullaby.

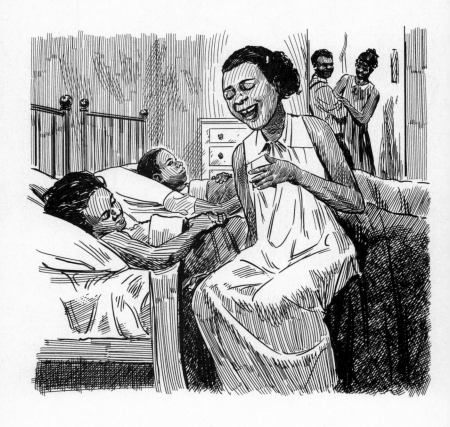

But Celia's lullabies never put them to sleep. The children always wanted to hear more! Neighbors started to gather outside the window each night. They wanted to listen, too. Celia's voice was already drawing crowds in the neighborhood.

Sometimes Celia's parents asked her to sing for their friends. Celia was shy, but she loved to sing so much that she got over it to perform. No one loved Celia's singing more than her cousin Serafín. He thought she was good enough to one day sing professionally. But such a dream seemed impossible for a poor Afro-Cuban girl from Havana.

Celia's parents were very protective. She wasn't allowed to go out by herself that often. She walked to school with her friends, and when she became a teenager, they went to school dances. But Celia longed to go to Carnival.

Every year during Carnival, the streets of Havana filled with people dancing and singing.

# Carnival

Carnival is a yearly celebration in Havana. It originated in medieval Italy. Carnival celebrates the time before the Catholic season of Lent. During Lent, Catholics are supposed to avoid eating meat, and sometimes they also choose to give up their favorite foods. So Carnival was a big party they had before Lent started.

Carnival has been celebrated in Havana since 1573. People paraded down the streets in costume, rode in carriages, and danced. When enslaved people were brought to Cuba, the black population eventually joined the parade, adding African instruments and dances.

When Celia was fourteen, she and some of her friends went to Carnival, but Celia didn't tell her parents. She knew that they didn't think it was safe. Her father, especially, thought that young girls might get into trouble by themselves, or even get lost in the crowd. But Celia had a wonderful time. When she got home, she felt very guilty for lying. So the next morning, she confessed what she'd done to her Tía Ana.

"If you promise not to go out again without an adult," her aunt said, "I'll take you." So Celia got to go back to Carnival the next night. When they got home, Celia's mother winked at them. She knew just where they'd been.

That night Celia had a dream in which she was the queen of Carnival. She saw herself wearing a flowing white gown, her hair pulled back in a bun and her head topped with a floral crown. When she awoke the next morning, she wondered if her dream could ever come true.

# CHAPTER 2
## Life Choices

Celia loved to sing, but she knew that when she grew up, she was going to be a teacher. That was her father's dream for her. Teaching was a good, respectable job. When Celia graduated from high school, she entered a teachers college in Havana.

Education in Cuba was free, so Celia did not have to pay to attend.

When she was twenty-two and still in school, she won first prize in a singing contest on the radio. Celia started entering other contests. And sometimes she won! Her prizes were small items like soap, chocolate bars, and condensed milk. To Celia, these gifts were valuable. Although there were some people in Cuba who were rich, most people were poor. It was hard to find jobs. Black Cubans like Celia and her family often had the lowest paying work. Celia's father was a railway worker who shoveled coal to power the trains.

He had to support a big family on his salary—not only his own four children and his wife but also many other relatives who lived with the family at different times.

When Celia won fifteen pesos (about eighty-nine cents at the time), she was thrilled. She used the money to buy the books she needed for her studies at the teachers college. Often Celia

didn't have enough money to take a trolley to the radio stations where the contests were held. The city of Havana covered over 280 square miles, and Celia traveled all over it. Sometimes she had to walk miles to get to a contest—or else pay for her fare by singing for the driver.

Celia's family was always excited when she was on the radio. Everyone but her father, that is. One day, he told her flat-out that he didn't like her decision to sing. Celia was hurt, but her mother said, "Don't pay attention to him . . . you just keep doing what you're doing and I'll deal with him."

Celia started singing with local bands and at parties. She often wasn't paid for these shows, but she liked performing. Once when Tía Ana watched her sing, she gave Celia some advice. She explained that the audience wanted to see everything Celia was feeling when she sang. She shouldn't use just her voice but her body as well. Celia stood still when she sang, like a flagpole. "Next time, I want to see you move," Tía Ana said. And Celia did start to move. She let the music flow through her and swayed with it.

When Celia graduated from the teachers college in 1949, she was very proud. After the ceremony, she went to one of her teachers and asked her advice about starting her career as a teacher. Her teacher said, "Celia, God gave you a wonderful gift. With the voice you have, you can make a good living. If you pursue a singing career, you'll be able to make in one day what it takes me one month to make. Don't waste your time trying to become a teacher. You were put on earth to make people happy—by using your gift."

Celia was surprised to hear her teacher speak that way. She was also thrilled. Could she really spend her life doing what she loved most? Yes! Right then, Celia decided to become a singer. She had no other choice than to follow her destiny.

# CHAPTER 3
## Stepping Out in the World

Celia took her new career very seriously. She started studying at the Havana Music Academy. Her piano teacher was a well-known composer, Oscar Muñoz Boufartique. Celia never learned to play the piano well. Her long nails got in the way. But she couldn't bear to cut them. In the end, it

didn't matter, because she didn't love playing the piano as much as she loved singing.

She tried hard to find work. Her cousin Serafín also looked for opportunities for her. When she was offered any job, Serafín made sure she was paid fairly. Thanks to all the contests she'd won, many radio shows hired her to sing. Celia would go to the CMQ studios in Havana, where radio shows were broadcast. She would sit on the bench in the reception area with all the other performers who had a job to do that day.

Celia spent many hours sitting on that bench, waiting. While she was there, she studied all the other performers to see what she could learn. Everyone was very nice and helpful to her.

Myrta Silva

She made a lot of great friends while sitting on the bench. The performers called it the "Bench of Dreams" because they spent so much time there imagining what their future might be. Celia often dreamed about performing with famous Cuban artists. One of her favorite groups was La Sonora Matancera (say: la son-OR-a ma-tahn-SARE-a). Their singer, Myrta Silva, was from Puerto Rico. Celia would have loved to sing with the group!

Celia did get the chance to perform with many other bands. In 1950, she even got to make a record for the first time with a group called Puchito. It wasn't a big hit, but recording was a fun, new experience.

One day, when she was twenty-five, Celia met a man named Roderico "Rodney" Neyra. He invited Celia to be part of an Afro-Cuban dance-and-music show called *Sun Sun BaBae*, which means "pretty bird of dawn." *Zun zun* (say: ZOON ZOON) is the name of a hummingbird native to Cuba. Celia was the main singer in the show, singing

Roderico "Rodney" Neyra

*guarachas* (say: gwa-RA-chas), a type of Cuban song.

The show was a big hit. It was first performed outside the city. Then it moved to the Tropicana nightclub in Marianao, a neighborhood on the west side of Havana. Celia thought the Tropicana was one of the most beautiful places she'd ever seen. The club was outdoors, with arches made of colored glass that shone under the stars.

Tropicana nightclub in Marianao, Havana

# Cuban Songs

The rhythms and instruments of Cuban music display the influence of many cultures, especially those from Spain and West Africa. It is very popular all over the world.

Some familiar types of Cuban songs are:

- Guaracha (say: gwa-RA-cha): a song that is funny and upbeat
- Bolero (say: bowl-AIR-o): a romantic, heartfelt, slower song
- Son (say: SONE): a song that combines the feel of Spanish songs with Afro-Cuban drums
- Guajira (say: gwa-HEAR-a): music from the countryside usually played on a six-string guitar called a tres
- Pregón (say: pray-GO-n): a traditional Cuban vendor's call set to music

Celia Cruz with Las Mulatas de Fuego

Rodney also created a dance troupe called Las Mulatas de Fuego, which means "the fiery mixed-race women." When the show was invited to tour in Venezuela and Mexico, Celia went with them as a singer. Growing up, she never imagined she would see the world outside of Cuba. Now she was flying on airplanes and traveling to other countries!

The more shows Celia did, the more she loved performing. But her father still wasn't happy about her career. He never told anyone that Celia was his daughter. Then one day at work, some of the other railway men were reading an article in the local newspaper. "Look, Simón," one of them said. "This girl has the same name as you."

Celia's father read the article. It was all about how talented Celia was. She was just as admired as a singer as he had imagined she would be as a teacher! From that day on, Celia's father was proud of his daughter, the singer.

# CHAPTER 4
## La Sonora Matancera

Although Celia was now a professional singer herself, she was still a big fan of her favorite group, La Sonora Matancera. It had been a popular group in Cuba for a long time. The name meant "the sound of Matancera"— the Cuban city of Matanzas. In 1950, it was announced that the band's singer, Myrta Silva, was leaving the group to return to her home country of Puerto Rico. The band wanted to audition Celia as a replacement! They had heard her sing on the radio.

Celia was excited—but nervous, too. When she got to the studio for her audition, the first person she saw was the group's trumpet player, Pedro Knight. He looked over the music that

Celia had brought to sing. Unfortunately, it had been written for a band of fourteen people, and Sonora Matancera had only nine. Their musical director agreed to change it to fit the band. The musicians wanted to hear what Celia could do, and were willing to help her do her best in the audition.

## Sonora Matancera

The band Sonora Matancera was founded on January 12, 1924 in Matanzas, Cuba, by Valentin Cané and Pablo "Bubu" Vázquez Gobin. Up until 1925, the group's Afro-Cuban style of music (songs that were influenced by African rhythms and culture) was not allowed to be played in many white clubs and hotels. But, over time, the band became popular with white audiences, too, including white

Cubans and white tourists visiting Cuba from other countries.

The musicians play a mix of popular dance music that includes the son, guaracha, bolero and many more forms. The band has had many members over the years and is still performing today. Throughout its career, Sonora Matancera has recorded over four thousand songs!

Celia went home to wait for the new music to be written. Two weeks passed. While she was waiting, an article was published in the newspaper that said that Myrta Silva was going to be replaced by Celia Cruz! But she hadn't even auditioned yet! She was still working at the radio station, and her boss fired her when he heard the announcement. Celia called the director of Sonora Matancera, Rogelio Martínez. He told her to come in for an audition. That audition got her the job.

Celia's very first performance with Sonora Matancera was on August 3, 1950. Her family was sitting in the front row. Being in the band was a dream come true for Celia, but some fans of Myrta Silva called the radio station and wrote angry letters, saying Celia's voice wasn't right for the band. Some of the letters really hurt Celia's feelings, but she concentrated on doing her job well. She learned all her songs, was always on time for rehearsal, and worked well with the band.

Sadly, not long after she began singing with Sonora Matancera, her beloved cousin Serafín died. Serafín had always believed in Celia's talent. She was sad that he would not get to see her become the star he always thought she could be.

Celia recorded two songs with the band that became big dance hits. She became more widely accepted as the voice of the group. In fact, people loved how passionate and strong her voice was. Others described it as being warm, like coffee with milk.

Celia and the band made a new record every three months. They toured together in Haiti, South America, and Mexico. Celia loved traveling with the band, and the band loved her. Some of them called her "Herma," short for *hermana*, which means "sister." They all treated her like they were her big brothers. If they were out at a club and anyone tried to bother her, the band would be right there to protect her.

Out of everyone in the band, Celia was closest to trumpet player Pedro Knight. Pedro had a lot of girlfriends, but Celia was his best friend.

When Celia wasn't singing with the band, she was recording short commercial songs for TV and radio ads. She didn't appear in the television commercials, though. At that time, only white people appeared on television.

So Celia's voice was dubbed—she made a recording of the song first, and then an actress lip-synched during the filming of the advertisement. Celia recorded short advertising songs for soap, rum, Coke, cigars, cheese, cologne, coffee, pineapple soda, and beer.

For the first time in her life, Celia was making enough money to help her family and also buy some things for fun. She had fans all over Cuba, and her music was played in many other countries, including the United States. Her life was becoming more exciting than she'd ever dreamed it could be—even better than being Carnival Queen!

# CHAPTER 5
# A New Cuba

In 1957, Celia got an exciting invitation. One of her records was a big hit in the United States, where Cuban music was becoming more popular. The song was called "Burundanga" (say: boo-roon-DONG-gah), which means "piece of junk." Producers wanted to award her a gold record for it. Celia went to New York City and performed her song. While she was there, she even appeared in a movie called *Affair in Havana*.

When Celia returned to Cuba, she got the bad news that her mother had cancer. Celia's father was also not well. Celia tried to help her parents any way she could. When she was growing up, there had never been much money for food—or anything else for that matter.

The economy in Cuba was very bad. Many families struggled to earn enough money to eat. But in 1959, a new leader of the country promised that he would make sure everyone had what they needed. His name was Fidel Castro.

Fidel Castro

# Revolution

In 1952, Fulgencio Batista, a former president of Cuba, canceled the country's elections and put himself into power. Many people thought that Batista did not care about the problems of many of the Cuban people. Jobs were scarce under his rule, and people struggled to earn money to buy food. Batista even said that US companies did not have to pay the same taxes as Cuban businesses did. Sometimes they didn't have to pay taxes at all. A small group of people got rich under Batista, but most people suffered.

A young lawyer and activist named Fidel Castro accused Batista of corruption. He started a petition to take him out of power. But Batista controlled

the courts and had the petition thrown out. So
Castro and his brother Raúl launched a revolution.
They raised a force of around twelve hundred
followers called the "26th of July Movement." They
gathered weapons and attacked military bases.
The Movement drove Batista and his supporters
out of the government in 1959. Fidel Castro and his
supporters were now in charge.

When the Castro government took control of Cuba, the new officials wanted to give more rights to poorer Cubans, black Cubans, and women. But they also wanted more control over the people. This meant less freedom for Cuban citizens, including artists like Celia. She did not trust the new leader. Once when she was performing at a party that Castro attended, she was told that he wanted to meet her. Celia preferred to stay by the piano. If Fidel Castro wanted to meet her, he would have to walk over to greet her like any other guest. Castro was not pleased. He was not used to people saying no to him.

Celia felt like the Castro government was trying to control everything—even people's personal lives. People could get into trouble for speaking against the government even in private. Everyone was afraid of being punished for not supporting the revolution.

Celia would not give in to that pressure.

Sometimes government agents knocked on the door at night. They had been ordered to bring Celia to perform for government officials. When this happened, she would hide while her brother, Bárbaro, nervously told the agents that she wasn't at home.

In July 1960, Sonora Matancera got a job performing in Mexico for a few weeks. Celia looked forward to being out of the country for a while. But she didn't want to be away long with both her parents so sick. In order to leave, the band members had to apply for exit visas.

These documents gave them permission to leave the country.

Celia and the band left Cuba on July 15, 1960. The whole family drove her to the airport, except for her father, who was too sick to go. As Celia got on the plane, she looked back and blew a kiss at her mother and Tía Ana outside.

After the plane had taken off, Rogelio, the band's manager, made an announcement. "Guys . . . ," he began. Celia could hear something was wrong. He looked her straight in the eye and said: "This is a one-way trip." Rogelio knew that if the band returned to Cuba, Castro would never allow any of them to leave again.

So, without telling the band, Rogelio had decided they had to flee for good.

Celia was in shock. She stared out the window. Her beloved Cuba was gone. She was thirty-four years old. She had left her family behind. And she might not ever see any of them again.

# CHAPTER 6
# No Turning Back

In Mexico City, Celia was heartbroken that she couldn't go home or see her family. Not long after the band arrived, Celia was able to call home and found out that her father had died. She wanted to go home to see her mother. But her mother said she should stay where she was. She didn't want Celia to return to Cuba.

In October, Fidel Castro announced that any Cuban person living abroad had to come home immediately if they wanted to continue to be a citizen of Cuba. Celia did not go home.

In 1961, Celia performed in Los Angeles. And when that job was over, she got a job in New York City. She decided to stay there. Many Latin musicians, singers, and fans lived in New York. She was later joined there by the members of both Sonora Matancera and Las Mulatas de Fuego. Together they toured other cities, including Miami and Chicago. In 1966, the US government announced that Cubans who had fled Castro's government could stay in the United States permanently.

Back in Cuba, Castro banned Celia's music from all radio stations. Since Celia had defied him and left the country, he wanted to erase her from Cuban culture and history. He believed that to listen to her sing was dangerous because others might follow her example, reject his leadership, and maybe want to leave Cuba.

US cities Celia toured in 1961

Celia enjoyed touring the United States, but she still worried about her family. She spoke to her mother and Tía Ana on the phone as often as she could. Her mother was getting weaker. Sometimes she was too tired to talk. But she never asked Celia to come to see her. She never wanted Celia to risk returning to Cuba.

Everyone in Sonora Matancera knew how much Celia missed her family and how she worried about her mother. They tried to cheer her up. As always, Pedro was her best friend. They spent more and more time together. Pedro lost interest in all the girlfriends that he used to go out with. He preferred to spend time with Celia. One day, twelve years after they had first met, Pedro told Celia he had a problem. "I think I'm falling in love with my best friend," he said.

"And why don't you tell your best friend what you're feeling?" she asked.

"Because I don't want to lose her friendship."

"But Pedro," Celia said, "if she's your best friend, don't you think she knows you well enough? Why should you have to lose her?"

Pedro took Celia's hand and kissed her for the first time. From that moment on, Celia knew her heart belonged to him.

# Fidel Castro (1926–2016)

Fidel Alejandro Castro Ruz was born near Birán, Cuba. His father was a wealthy farmer. Fidel studied law at the University of Havana. There, he joined student groups with members who thought the government should be overthrown. Fidel led an attack on an army barracks on July 26, 1953. He was arrested and jailed for over a year. When he got out, he went to Mexico and formed the 26th of July Movement with his brother Raúl and friend Che Guevara. He played a key role in the Cuban Revolution. And when it ended, he became the prime minister of Cuba in 1959. In 1976, he also became the president of Cuba after the adoption of a new Cuban constitution.

He held both positions until he retired in 2008. He died in Cuba on November 25, 2016.

On April 7, 1962, Celia was preparing to perform with Sonora Matancera at the Teatro Puerto Rico in New York City. Coming back from getting her nails done, she heard Pedro talking to someone on the phone. She overheard him say, "Look, Celia's mother passed away last night but she still doesn't know."

Pedro had just gotten the news and was trying
to figure out how to tell her.

Celia ran out of the room. Pedro ran after her.
"I didn't want you to suffer so much," he said.
Celia still performed in the show that night. She
didn't want to disappoint the audience. But she
cried in between the songs.

Celia made a request to the Cuban government to be allowed to go home for her mother's funeral. But Fidel Castro had never forgiven her for defying him by leaving the country. He did not like anyone who challenged him, especially when they won. He denied her request. Celia would never forgive him, either.

# CHAPTER 7
## Celia and Tito

Just a few months after her mother's death, Celia became the first Latina to perform at Carnegie Hall, one of the most famous concert halls in New York City. She performed with another Latin star, Tito Puente.

# Latino or Hispanic?

*Latino/Latina/Latinx* and *Hispanic* are words often used to describe people from Cuba. Many people think these words mean the same thing, but they don't.

*Latino*, *Latina*, and *Latinx* are terms that refer to the place where someone or someone's family is from. Each means they are from Latin America. Latin America includes all the Spanish-speaking countries in North, Central, and South America.

*Hispanic* refers to the language of Spanish. If a person or their family comes from a place where Spanish is spoken, they are said to be Hispanic.

There is a lot of overlap between the two groups. But they are not the same. A person from Spain is Hispanic because they speak Spanish. But they are not Latino because Spain is in Europe. A person from Brazil is Latino because Brazil is in

Latin America. But they are not Hispanic because Portuguese is spoken in Brazil.

Celia was both Hispanic and Latina.

Spanish-speaking countries

On July 14, 1962, Celia and Pedro were married in Greenwich, Connecticut. Celia said: "Pedro, you're my friend, my brother, my cousin. You are the only family I have left." It was a small ceremony, with just Celia, Pedro, and three close friends present.

But the following year, Celia's sister Gladys got permission from the Cuban government to travel to Mexico. Once she arrived, Pedro and Celia arranged for her to come and live in the United States. Celia was thrilled to have at least one person from her family with her in New York.

Celia was getting more and more popular in the United States. By 1965, she had been singing with Sonora Matancera for fifteen years! She wanted to try something new. So Celia left the band to work with Tito Puente.

Pedro agreed with Celia's decision to leave Sonora Matancera. In fact, he left, too. Celia traveled with Pedro all over the United States and Latin America. She loved performing with Tito and other Latin singers, especially fellow Cuban exiles—other people who also had been barred from returning to Cuba.

# Tito Puente (1923–2000)

Ernesto Antonio "Tito" Puente was born in New York City. His parents were immigrants from Puerto Rico. He grew up in the neighborhood called Spanish Harlem. When Tito's neighbors complained that seven-year-old Tito was always making noise by banging on pots and pans, his mother took him to a piano teacher. By age ten, he had switched to drumming. He served in the navy during World War II and then studied music at The Juilliard School in New York. In the 1950s, he started introducing Afro-Cuban and Caribbean music to American audiences and was sometimes called "The Kettledrum King" and "The King of Latin Music."

But Celia was uncomfortable performing with Cuban artists who still lived in Cuba and supported the Castro government. Castro gave these artists permission to leave Cuba to perform in other countries and then return to Cuba. Celia refused to play on the same stage with them. She did not want to use her popularity to earn money that would go back to support Castro. It was as simple as that.

# CHAPTER 8
## *Azúcar!*

Celia performed traditional types of songs from different Latin countries. She had been performing for many years now, and when she looked out at the audience, she noticed that everyone seemed older. And the audiences were getting smaller. Was Celia's music too old-fashioned?

Young people in the 1970s were more interested in rock 'n' roll and dance music, like disco. Latin or Hispanic people knew who Celia Cruz was. She was famous all over the Spanish-speaking world. Their parents not only loved her music but Celia herself. But for young people in America, this music was something for the older generation. Cuban music wasn't considered cool.

# Traditional Latin Songs

There are many countries in Latin America and the Caribbean. Each one has its own musical tradition:

- Colombian Cumbia (say: KOOM-bee-ah): This style of music started as a courtship dance among the African population on the coasts of Panama and Colombia.

- Puerto Rican bomba (say: BOHM-ba): Bomba is a mixture of three different cultures from Puerto Rico: African, Spanish, and Taino. Bomba players try to connect dancers to the beat of the drummer.

- Dominican merengue (say: meh-REN-gay): Meringue first appeared in the Caribbean in the 1850s. It was played on stringed instruments and then the accordion.

Dominican merengue

- **Mexican ranchero (say: rahn-CHAIR-oh): This style draws on Mexican folk music. The traditional subjects in the songs were love, patriotism, and nature.**

- **Mexican corrido (say: core-REE-doh): This type of song tells a story about history or the daily life of working people. Before television and radio, many people got their news by listening to corridos.**

If the younger generation wanted something new, Celia didn't see why she couldn't *be* something new while still being herself. She started to work with a famous Dominican flutist named Johnny Pacheco. In 1964, Johnny started a record company for a new kind of Latin music called salsa. It included the traditional music of many different countries and styles but was played with more contemporary electronic instruments. Salsa sounded modern. It made people move to the beat.

Celia could sing the songs she loved while also experimenting with new styles like disco. In 1974, she and Johnny released a single called "Químbara" (say: KEEM-bara) that was a big hit. *Quimbara* was a made-up word based on the name of an African god.

# Johnny Pacheco (1935–)

Juan "Johnny" Azarías Pacheco Kiniping was born on March 25, 1935, in Santiago de los Caballeros, Dominican Republic. His father was a bandleader. When he was eleven, his family moved to New York City. Johnny studied the accordion, violin, flute, saxophone, and clarinet. He formed his own band in 1959.

In 1964, he started Fania Records with music promoter Jerry Masucci, and then came up with the word *salsa* to describe a new kind of music. In 1968, he became the musical director of the Fania All-Stars band to showcase the performers on the record label. He has recorded and composed over 150 songs, and is one of the most influential musicians in Latin music.

The song was about doing a dance called the rumba. In English, the words meant: "Oh, if you wanna have fun, you wanna dance, Quimbara, cumbara cumba-quimbambá!"

Salsa was played in nightclubs and was great for dancing. Some Latin performers, such as Tito Puente, never liked this new musical word, which was also the name of a spicy sauce. Tito made Celia laugh when he said: "You eat salsa, you don't dance to it."

As the top female performer with Fania Records, Celia became known as the Queen of Salsa. Along with "Quimbara," she had big hits with songs like "Toro mata" (The Bull Kills) and "Cúcala" (Cuckoo). She loved the word *salsa*. Anything that made people dance to her beloved Cuban music was dear to her heart—and young people loved salsa. It was all about the beat. Once again, Celia's concerts were sold out.

Celia was becoming famous not only for her salsa music but also for her sugar! In Spanish, sugar is called *azúcar* (say: ah-SOO-car). At one performance, before singing, Celia told a story about being in a Miami café drinking coffee. The waiter asked if she would like sugar. She said of course she would—she was Cuban! Cubans always took sugar in their coffee. Her fans loved the story so much, she started telling it over and over. Eventually, she would just shout *Azúcar!* before she began to sing. For her the word meant everything she loved about Cuba and being Cuban.

The beat of Celia's salsa music was not that different from the beat of disco music. Both were played in nightclubs where people went to dance. Celia fit perfectly into the world of disco. It was glamorous and flashy and fun. The floors of a disco lit up under the dancers' feet. Light

reflecting off rotating mirrored balls hanging from the ceilings flashed on the walls.

Celia wore bright-colored dresses with sequins

and fancy wigs and heavy makeup. She felt the world had finally caught up to her Carnival dream and crowned her queen.

# CHAPTER 9
## Citizen of the World

In the fall of 1974, Celia traveled to Africa for the first time. The trip meant a lot to her since her ancestors were enslaved and taken from Africa to Cuba. When Celia got off the plane in the Republic of Zaire (now known as the Democratic Republic of the Congo), she collected a handful

of soil in a plastic bag for a souvenir. Celia and Johnny Pacheco were there to perform before a boxing match between Muhammad Ali and George Foreman.

Lourdes Aguila

On her way home from Africa, Celia met Lourdes Aguila in Miami. Lourdes worked for a charity that raised money for cancer research. The group put on a telethon every year as a fundraiser. Because her own mother had died from cancer, Celia promised not only to perform in the telethon that year but also every year after that.

# The "Rumble in the Jungle"

In 1974, George Foreman was the heavyweight boxing champion of the world. Muhammad Ali, a former champion, wanted to win the title back. On October 30, 1974, the two fighters met in Kinshasa, the capital of Zaire. The event drew worldwide attention and had a three-day music festival before the day of the fight, which was held at 4:00 a.m. so that people in other countries could watch it live on television. About 60,000 people attended the boxing match in person. Ali won the fight, knocking out Foreman in the eighth round. Nicknamed the "Rumble in the Jungle" the fight has been called "the greatest sporting event of the twentieth century."

Muhammad Ali punches his opponent, George Foreman

During the telethon in 1977, Celia performed with a band called Miami Sound Machine. In Miami, she got to know the lead singer, Gloria Estefan, and her husband, Emilio, a Cuban-born musician, singer, and producer.

Celia and Pedro had been permanent residents of the United States for many years. But in 1977,

they officially became citizens. They attended a
swearing-in ceremony in a downtown Brooklyn
courthouse. Celia was so happy to have her papers
that she shouted with joy, and a policeman ran up
to her, thinking she was in trouble! New York had
welcomed Celia as one of its own, and she loved
the city for it.

# Gloria Estefan

Gloria María Milagrosa Fajardo García was born on September 1, 1957, in Havana, Cuba. Her family fled to the United States when she was a young child. She grew up in Miami and became the lead singer of Miami Sound Machine. In 1978, she married the band's leader, Emilio Estefan, and became known as Gloria Estefan.

The group had its first big hit with the song "Conga" in 1985. Other hits include "Anything for You," "1-2-3," and "Rhythm Is Gonna Get You." In 1990, Gloria was seriously injured when the group's tour bus crashed, but she recovered and started performing again less than six months later. In 2015, the Broadway musical *On Your Feet!* (based on the lives of Gloria and Emilio) premiered in New York City.

In 1982, Celia was back in Miami, performing for the telethon. During the long night of fundraising, she got a phone call from a stranger— a twelve-year-old boy. His name was Luisito Falcón. He told Celia that his aunt was a big fan of hers, and he had become one, too. A friend of his mother had told him where Celia was staying, so Luisito called the hotel and asked to be connected by phone to her room.

Celia was happy to talk to Luisito even though he had called her late at night. From then on, she and Luisito talked on the phone often. She sent him postcards from wherever she was performing. She told him to send her all his report cards so she could be sure he was keeping up with his schoolwork. Celia and Luisito didn't meet in person until a year later.

In 1985, Celia went to a Christmas party where she met fourteen-year-old Omer Pardillo-Cid. Omer had been a fan since he was six years old and living in Cuba. Because Celia's music was banned from the radio there, Omer listened to her records that people had kept in secret.

Even though Castro had tried to make the people of Cuba forget Celia, they had held her close to their hearts. Her music lived on. Celia was so proud of the brave people in her country for listening to the music they loved—and for not forgetting her. Not only did they keep her old records, they also managed to smuggle new recordings into the country.

Celia and Pedro never had children of their own. But Omer and Luisito became like family—like the sons they never had.

In 1987, Celia was honored with a star on the Hollywood Walk of Fame. The Walk of Fame is a fifteen-block stretch of Hollywood Boulevard and three blocks along Vine Street in Los Angeles where famous performers are honored with stars embedded in the sidewalk.

And the following year. Celia was named grand marshal of the Puerto Rican Day Parade in New York City. The parade is an annual event that is very important to Puerto Ricans. It often also honors other Latin and Hispanic performers. As a girl growing up in Havana, Celia had dreamed of being queen of Carnival, but even she could not have imagined leading such a big parade celebrating Latin culture and music in the United States!

# CHAPTER 10
## Celia Forever

In 1992, Celia was featured in the movie *The Mambo Kings*. She played a club owner who was also a singer and fortune-teller. Right after filming *The Mambo Kings*, she was offered a part in another movie, *The Perez Family*, about a group of Cuban refugees in the United States.

Celia also appeared in telenovelas.

# Telenovelas

Telenovelas are TV shows whose stories play out over many episodes. They are produced in numerous countries in Latin America but have also become popular all over the world. They are known for having surprising plot twists and plenty of romance. They are much like American soap operas, but they rarely continue for more than a year. One of the most popular telenovelas was *Yo soy Betty, la fea* (I Am Betty, the Ugly One). The original version was filmed in Colombia and aired from 1999 to 2001, but it has since been remade in nineteen countries. In the United States *Ugly Betty* ran from 2006–2010.

Celia played a fortune-teller once again in *Valentina*, a 1993 telenovela that was filmed in Mexico City. The series was a hit all over the world. Celia couldn't believe it when she heard the show was even shown in Russia. She couldn't imagine how her character would sound speaking Russian!

Celia Cruz as Lecumé in the telenovela *Valentina*

Celia later appeared in another series called *Souls Don't Have a Race*; she played the black mother of a woman who passed as white. Celia was proud of being in a series that told a story about racism.

As the twentieth century came to a close, in 1999, Celia recorded her seventy-sixth album,  *Celia Cruz and Friends: A Night of Salsa*. The following year brought joy and sadness. Her brother, Bárbaro, was able to come to New York for a visit. Sadly, both her good friend Tito Puente and beloved Tía Ana died that same year.

In June, Celia's salsa album won a Grammy Award. She performed at the awards show wearing a bright blue wig. Celia liked it so much, she started wearing candy-colored wigs a lot.

She wore an orange wig to make a rap-salsa
video for a song called "La Negra Tiene Tumbao"
(say: la NAY-gra tee-en-ay toom-BOW), which
means "the black woman has the beat." Celia had
never worked with rappers before, but her brand
of salsa was a natural fit with their modern sound.

Music video for "La Negra Tiene Tumbao"

She sang words that in English mean: "The black woman walks with grace and doesn't get pushed aside."

Celia had been a star for over fifty years. Many people in the industry wanted to honor her for her years of bringing joy to others. *Billboard* magazine did a special tribute issue for Celia.

Her "La Negra Tiene Tumbao" salsa-rap song was nominated for four Latin Grammys: best record and best video, and the album of the same title was nominated as album of the year and won for best salsa album.

Celia Cruz performs "La Negra Tiene Tumbao" at the Latin Grammys

In November 2002, Celia and Pedro traveled to Mexico for a tribute concert called the Fiftieth Anniversary of Celia Cruz's Musical Career. Pedro surprised Celia by joining her onstage to sing a duet. Celia was thrilled but suddenly felt very tired. She had trouble remembering the words of the song. She knew something was wrong.

The couple flew back to New York and Celia went to the doctor. She learned she had a brain tumor. She made a statement to the press thanking her fans for being so loyal. She told them she was sick but did not share all the details. She spent most of her time surrounded by the people she loved: Pedro, Gladys, Omer, Luisito, and cousins and friends in the United States.

Even though she was sick, Celia wanted to do what she loved: sing. She started work on a new album, *Regalo del Alma* (Gift of the Soul). She was even able to travel to Miami in February 2003 for a big tribute concert to her hosted by Telemundo, the American- and Spanish-language television network. Dozens of stars performed, including Gloria and Emilio Estefan, and disco queen Gloria Gaynor.

After the concert, Celia and Pedro returned home to New York. She became weaker and weaker, but was always happy when friends came to see her.

On July 13, 2003, she received copies of the first few songs she had recorded for the new album.

July 14, 2003, was Celia and Pedro's forty-first wedding anniversary. By then, Celia was very weak. Pedro asked her if she knew what day it was. She couldn't speak, but a tear ran down her face. She did know.

Celia died at home two days later. Funerals were held for her both in New York and Miami, two cities that had claimed her as their own. All across Cuba, masses were said in her honor. Graffiti started to appear around the country. Just one word: *Azúcar!*

Fidel Castro sent the police to clean the words off. But every time they did, more *azúcars* appeared. Castro couldn't silence Celia's fans any more than he could silence her.

Celia Cruz never had the chance to live in Cuba again. But in 1990, she performed for American soldiers at Guantánamo Bay Naval Base, a US detention camp that sits on a piece of land that belongs to Cuba. When Celia came to Guantánamo, she kissed the ground and said, "I have kissed the earth in the name of all the Cubans in exile." Celia may have left Cuba,

but the people of Cuba kept her in their hearts.
Even more, she brought the heart of Cuba to the
whole world.

*Azúcar!*

# Timeline of Celia Cruz's Life

| | |
|---|---|
| **1925** — | Celia Cruz is born in Havana, Cuba, on October 21 |
| **1947** — | Enrolls in Escuela Normal para Maestros, a teachers college in Havana |
| **1950** — | Joins La Sonora Matancera |
| **1957** — | Visits the United States for the first time |
| **1960** — | Leaves Cuba forever, on July 15 |
| **1962** — | Marries Pedro Knight |
| **1965** — | Starts working steadily with Tito Puente |
| **1972** — | Performs at Radio City Music Hall with other Cuban exiles |
| **1974** — | Performs in Zaire, Africa, as part of the "Rumble in the Jungle" boxing match |
| **1977** — | Becomes a US citizen |
| **1986** — | Wins her first Grammy, for Best Tropical Latin Performance, with her album *Ritmo En El Corazón* |
| **1987** — | Gets a star on the Hollywood Walk of Fame |
| **1988** — | Appears on a *Sesame Street* special |
| **1992** — | Appears in the movie *The Mambo Kings* |
| **1993** — | Appears in the telenovela *Valentina* |
| **2003** — | Dies in Fort Lee, New Jersey, on July 16 |

# Timeline of the World

1925 — First issue of the magazine *The New Yorker* is published, on February 21

1929 — Popeye the Sailor character first appears in a newspaper comic strip

1933 — First drive-in movie theater opens, in Camden, New Jersey

1938 — Oil is discovered in Saudi Arabia

1946 — The first bikinis go on sale in France

1948 — Israel is declared an independent state

1953 — Sir Edmund Hillary and Tenzing Norgay become the first people to reach the summit of Mount Everest, on May 29

1969 — Neil Armstrong becomes the first person to walk on the moon, on July 20

1978 — First Susan B. Anthony dollar coin is minted in the United States

1985 — Microsoft releases the first version of Windows

1989 — *The Simpsons* premieres, on December 17

1993 — The World Wide Web is developed in Switzerland

2004 — The United States successfully lands two exploration robots on Mars

# Bibliography

**\*Books for young readers**

\*Brown, Monica, illustrated by Rafael López. *My Name Is Celia: The Life of Celia Cruz.* Flagstaff, AZ: Rising Moon, 2004.

\*Chambers, Veronica, illustrated by Julie Maren. *Celia Cruz, Queen of Salsa.* New York: Dial Books for Young Readers, 2005.

*Celia Cruz, An Extraordinary Woman . . . Azúcar!*, DVD, 2003.

*Celia the Queen*, DVD, 2009.

Cruz, Celia, with Ana Christina Reymundo. *Celia: My Life: An Autobiography.* New York: HarperCollins, 2004.

\*Da Coll, Ivar. *Azúcar!* New York: Lectorum Publications, 2005.

Farber, Samuel. "Cuba Before the Revolution." *Jacobin*, September 6, 2015. https://www.jacobinmag.com/2015/09/cuban-revolution-fidel-castro-casinos-batista.

LaHabana.com. "A History of the Havana Carnival from 1573 to Today." 2018. http://www.lahabana.com/Vintage/article_tropicana.php?id=The-Havana-Carnival-1573-to-2012.

Marceles, Eduardo. *Azúcar! The Biography of Celia Cruz.* New York: Reed Press, 2004.

Rodriguez-Duarte, Alexis. *Presenting Celia Cruz.* New York: Clarkson Potter, 2004.

\*Sciurba, Katie, illustrated by Edel Rodriguez. *Oye, Celia! A Song for Celia Cruz.* New York: Henry Holt, 2007.